Dream Wheels
– for Self-growth, Humanity & the World
by Della Burford

© Della Burford 2012
All rights for images belong
to the respective artists
"We come together to dream"

Editing: Dale Bertrand
Jacquie Howardson

ISBN 978-0-9878302-2-7
Azatlan Publishing

http://www.dellaburford.com
http://spiritofwritingandart.com

Contact Della:
dellaburford@hotmail.com

Brooklyn Academy of Music

Smithsonian Institute D.C.

'Magic in Me' Guatemala

Testimonial from Philip Rubinov Jacobson

"Della's book of words and images is an autobiographical account that bridges the beauty and wisdom of the collective unconscious with our waking life. It therefore serves as a guide for all of us to delve deeper into the realm of Dreamland where the colors and textures of feeling and fantasy can furnish us with a tapestry of spiritual insight and guidance. Della gives us a way to look behind the veil from which all forms spring from a Great Nothingness. It is in the dream state that an energetic exchange occurs, which is a direct experience of divine energy interfacing with and regenerating the process of individuation in the dreamer. It is a mystical experience."

"Della's story illustrates how the personal mind creates a bridge between divine unity and waking reality. Simply put, the mind writes a story to serve as this integral bridge. The story, which is really a metaphor for the unfolding of an experience of enlightenment, is what we call the "dream." Dreaming is indeed paradoxical but at the same time it can escape the entrapment of mind's dual nature. In its highest form, a dream occurs outside the comprehension of the individuated human. In its literal sense, it is written by the individuated mind. In its finest sense, a dream is entirely impersonal and is about Life and not about the personality of the dreamer. In its literal sense, it's a personal story. It is a story that transcends, includes and bridges all that is human with the enlightened mind and this book is a road map for that extraordinary adventure."

Philip Rubinov Jacobson,
Artist, Author and Teacher

Index for "Dream Wheels

Introduction

I have collected meaningful dreams and
recorded them in my diary, and created
40 Dream Wheels as a form of celebration
and a way of honoring my dreams for four decades
or forty years. The symbols and/or title on dreams in
the Dream Wheels becomes a portal back to the dreams
themselves and each year I read them all.

There are over 2000 dream segments recorded
in these wheels. I took them to Mexico and painted
Seven Wheels, each with a span of seven years and
each with approximately twenty dreams on it.
I found that each 7 years had a theme and were visual
pointers of obvious cycles of my life. I then did Dream
Collages showing the relationship of my dreams
and how they were manifested in real life such
as paintings, writings, books songs or plays. Now each
Dream Theme has become a mische painting.
My dreams help show me what is important
for my soul and spirit in life and what to focus on.
Dale and I studied with a shaman who also was a student
of Dr. Carl Jung and he helped us in many ways and
me to understand how to take my dreams to new levels.

Sometimes traumatic situations with divine limitations seem to be set but can become an opportunity to gain wisdom and healing. In one such incident in 1971 I saw the vision of the Bird Helmet which was a healing caduceus for me. Later this was put on my head and was used for travelling in the story 'Journey to Dodoland'. My mother and father even made me a Bird Helmet from the caduceus design which I wore for storytelling and I storytold with it on to thousands of children. New places can come from dreams as did many parts of the 'Journey to Dodoland' story. This story has now been shared by thousands of children and adults in theatre, music and on the internet by a million people. My dream became a world dream.

Threat of death can bring metamorphosis. This happened to me when I was twice fighting cancer, and it became a chance to change a problem to an opportunity. In these situations I created 'Journey to a Lotus', a book of poems and paintings and later the "Miracle Galaxy". The planet described in the "Miracle Galaxy" came from a dream. This story and art has been shared with thousands of cancer patients.

Dreams can guide you, as did one dream I had of little people who had a message "to love and take care of our planet" and this became the essence of 'Magical Earth Secrets.' It started as a personal myth that became a mythic journey for everyone. Dream Sacred beings and Angels can come alive. I was told in a dream to do dream work with others, and I am honoring that dream by writing this book. When we create from dreams we become artists of consciousness. This is why I included the last section of this book called 'Intentions' with the art work of various international artists who I met the summer of 2012. I feel they represent creativity and are living and painting in a conscious way with a world vision in mind.

It is important today in a time when we are more technologically capable to remember our own consciousness and compassion which are beyond what machines can do.
We can tune into our dreams and use our dreams in creative ways for self growth, humanity and the world. Remember your dreams, create from them and then share them with the world. Try it and you can make a difference and change the world!
Take care Namaste ....

MAKE Your Own DREAM WHEEL!
FOR A YEAR OR A MONTH.

THE DREAM WHEELS HAVE THREE RINGS.

THE CENTER RING IS IMPORTANT EVERYDAY
EVENTS FOLLOWING THE SEASONS.

THE OUTER RING IS DREAMS THAT ARE
CREATIVE, INSPIRATIONAL AND WISE DREAMS.
YOU CAN WRITE A TITLE FOR THE DREAM.

THE MIDDLE RING IS SMALL DRAWINGS
WHICH ARE SYMBOLS AND LIKE THE TITLE
REMINDS YOU OF THE DREAM AND
IS A PORTAL TO RETURN.

For thirty six years .. since 1976 I have
drawn Dream Wheels of my dreams for the year.
I have recorded 2000 lucid dream segments to 2012.

I have studied my thirty six years of
Dream Wheels (2000 dream segments) and
to make things more manageable have
divided them into Seven Year Cycles.
In these Seven Year Cycles I have chosen
twenty dreams to share in each which have
been manifested into art, writings, and plays.

Birth Cycle

Medicine Cycle

Wonder Cycle Wheel

Miracle Cycle Wheel

Flying

Theme Dream Wheels were painted in Mexico. These were like sketches really that were then each painted into "mische" style painting for the Theme Cycles. This photo is painting in Austria on the Dream Wheels. Each Theme Dream Wheel is now an oil and egg tempera canvas. Some are also done with acrylic and egg tempera which when painting inside was more environmentally friendly.

Painting in Mexico

Below you see the beach in the little town we were
in called Los Ayala. On the right are the Bird Men of
Papantl who were an inspiration. On the bottom
left are the Dream Theme sketches with watercolor.
On the bottom right is Hilda from "Artensanias Watakame"
who is friends with many Huichole artists. She told me how
she felt my symbols in the Dream Wheels related to the symbols
in their spiritual art. I love the Huichole art so was really
fascinated by her observations.

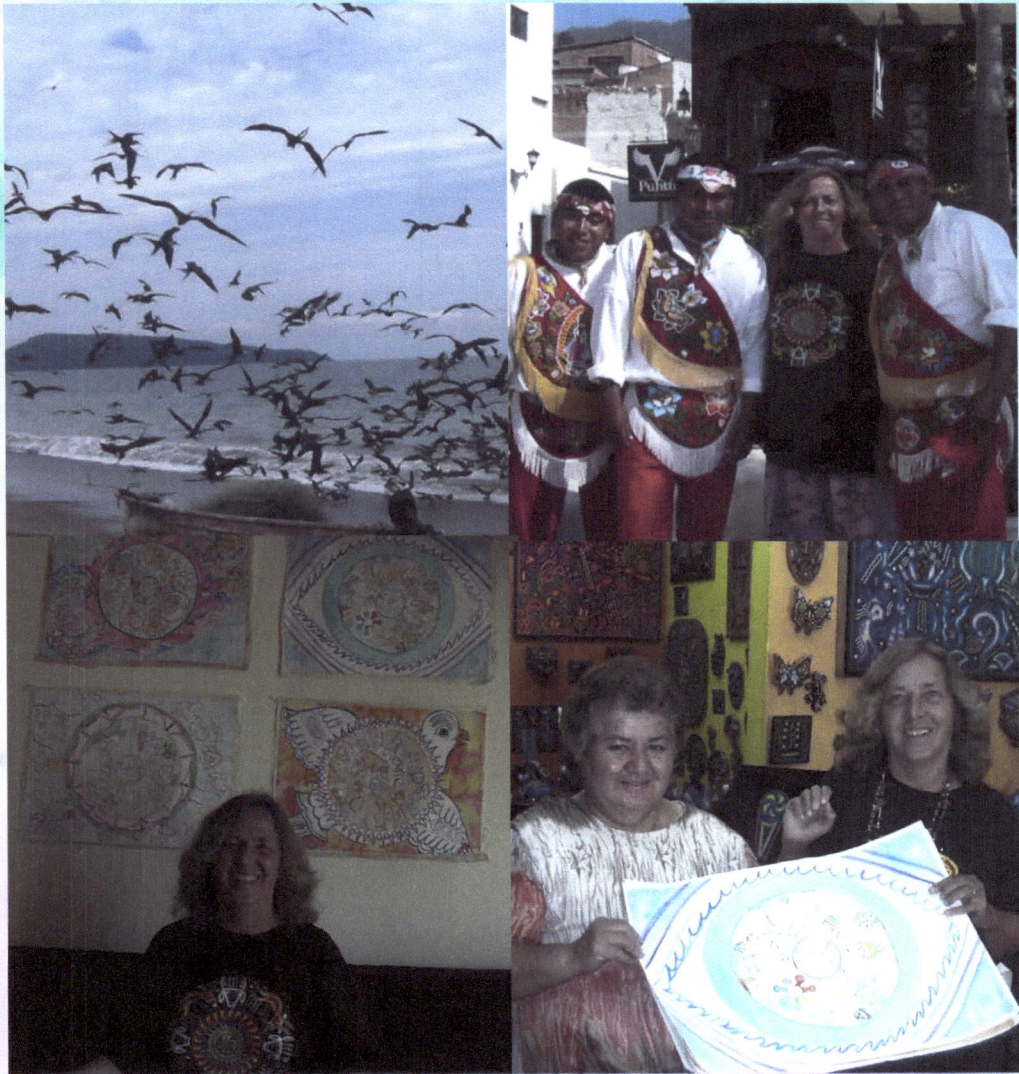

Painting in Austria and Bali

From a dream of Ernst Fuchs I decided to go to Austria in the summer of 2012 to learn the Mische painting technique -an Old Master technique from Philip Rubinov Jacobson whose mentor is Ernst Fuchs. I studied and met many fantastic artists and some became part of the "Dream Wheels" book. I also went on a pilgrimage to the Ernst Fuchs chapel in Klagenfurt. In 2012 my sister Norah coordinated a "Spirit of Painting" retreat at Balipurnati in which Prof Phil taught painting and myself an Inspiration class to many international artists. In 2014 we will have the Retreat at Wayan Karja's Santra Putra and he and I have a "Dream Wheels" show at the Karja Art Space.

Painting in the Garden– Vancouver Island

Also from the "Theme Dream Wheels" sketches I created 5 paintings in the summer of 2013 . I started with abstract grounds originally taught by my mum and used an adapted Mishe technique with red and yellow veils of paint with white tempera in between & then final color glazes. I studied photos of family and my twin for the "Miracle" painting. A workshop with Dream Shaman Robert Moss helped me finish the "Wonder" painting. A friend Janet looks on at the blue "Third Eye" painting painted in the full moon of August and September.

KEEP A DREAM DIARY.
RECORD REAL LIFE EVENTS AND DREAMS.

BELOW I HAVE REFLECTIONS FROM MY OWN
DIARIES aND DREAM WHEELS SHOWING
HOW I CREATED MY ART/WRITING
BY USING MY. DREAMS AS INSPIRATION.

MY WISH IN SHARING THIS IS FOR THIS TO BE
AN INSPIRATION FOR YOU TO START YOUR
OWN DREAM DIARY, WRITE DOWN 'YOUR DREAMS'
AND CREATE FROM YOUR DREAMS AND SHARE THEM!

AS I WENT THROUGH MY WHEELS
I DISCOVERED WHAT BECAME 'MY DREAMS' IN SHARING
BECAME 'OUR DREAMS' OR DREAMS FOR THE WORLD.

Reflection from Diaries – First Cycle – 1967–1973
The main theme of the first Cycle is Initiation

"You can find freedom in your dreams."

   This period I call Initiation as I feel it was a rite of
passage which prepared me for the privileges of the future.
Dale and I moved to Toronto in 1968 from Alberta. We felt
we were twin flames even at this time when we were sixteen
and seventeen. Since being a child I always painted with
my mother who was an artist. Even though later we were not
in the same city we were still very close. In Toronto Dale and I
worked and saved to travel for a year in Europe. We bought
a van and travelled, camped and visited many galleries,
saw the countryside and met many new friends. We were
questioning the values we saw in the world and feeling
a crisis of consciousness so we were looking for new directions.

   It is through unfortunate incidents we sometimes accelerate
forward. In 1971, while travelling to a foreign country, a traumatic
event happened Because of this I was alone in a room for one month .
Later I felt this was divine limitation as it became a creative
incubator for me. I am going to focus on the good. The good thing

that happened is that I discovered a new part of my inner self and had my first rememberance of dream recall and drew my dreams. In my dreams I was gifted with the birth of a magical mer-child, a flying mer-woman and a caduceus. I painted and drew a series from both my imagination and dreams. The paintings started with me inside of a cage and breaking free to run to a rainbow in the hills beyond. All I could think of was freedom. I felt my dreams and imagination were the only things I had left. I had a window where the birds would come to sing. I dreamed and drew what became the Bird Helmet as a healing caduceus which I felt later I had received as a gift from the Dream Temple of Asclepius – I became like Isis carrying the caduceus. This gift of a vision represented to me new life and later became in my first book the symbol that became the Bird Helmet for travelling.

Returning to Canada I started teaching Interior Design at Humber College and I continued to paint and write as well. In the summer of 1973, Dale and I travelled to India. Just before going I had a brush with cancer so when facing my own mortality or is it immortality many inspirations came. Divine limitation of my physical body brought dreams of transformation. While travelling I wrote many of the poems that became the blueprint for "Journey to a Lotus", forty years later published as a series of poems and paintings. I loved the rich culture of India and had many dreams and revelations about Buddha, the lotus, humanity and the world, and had an intense mystical experience that 'All is one'. Dreams and revelations became poems. One ,"Listen to the birds sing", became the secret to go to Dodoland.

Back from India I created the first painting that became part of the "Journey to Dodoland" – a story of travelling with a Bird Helmet, This had its origins in the healing caduceus that came in a vision and I called the painting 'Sea of Yourself'. I was travelling to a magical land where all dreams are possible and wearing my Bird Helmet. This land in the painting became a land called Dodoland. It was named this because one day a magical creature seemed to come out of the abstract ground I was doing in my Markham Street studio. He looked part Dodo bird and seemed to be other creatures like a fish, dragon and camel. The story developed that he had left earth as he was not treated well and found this land where he could be whatever he wanted to be- soon to be the dream of all that came to "Dodoland" to feel your freedom and live your dream. In 1978 my mother and father did something awesome for me – they made a real Bird Helmet for me to wear for storytelling.

Initiation Dream Cycle 1967-73

Top rows - Della & Desiree (mother) ..Paintings from "creative incubator"
including caduceus Lower- Dale & Della India - 'Journey to a Lotus' paintings

Inception of New Creations!

Initiation Dream Cycle 1967–73

"Flying Merbird" ink & watercolor December 1971.

In your Dreams you find Initiation
A divinely limited solitary room becomes creative incubation
You dream journey to the Dream Temple of Asclepius
Where you are given a Caduceus
Carrying the staff of Isis you find a purpose to live
You wear the Bird Helmet with power and possibilities
And Merbird is born and freedom is regained
Reminded that beyond the distant hills is a Rainbow
In your Dreams you find with your Bird Helmet you can fly

Reflections from Diaries/Dream Wheels – Second Cycle – 1974-1980–
The main theme of the Second Cycle was Birth.

"You can become what you want to be"

I call this the Birth cycle as it was the time of the birth of our first book which was like a first child – "Journey to Dodoland". In the early 1970's I had many dreams that became part of the book, such as the Crystal Cup which could go faster than the speed of light and became the way of travelling to Dodoland and the Singing Tree which was an "All is One" tree where everyone sat of all ages and as they sang different songs it turned different colors. I asked my friends what animal they would like to become, if they were in a fantasy story. They chose their favourite 'power animals' and thus the Dragon Ship evolved. The Dragon Ship has a Rainbow Dolphin (Dale), Giraffe (Loosie), Baby Panda (Tom), Seeing Eye Butterfly (Sal), Brigadier Lion (George), Pussycat (Shirley), Dancing Bear (John), Half Past Seven Beaver (Virgil), and Freddy the Frog (Bob), Wonder Walrus- Owl (Bruce), Dancing Flamingo (Ava) and many others. They became their myth. The elephants I loved in India got new life with the character Flutter Flump (Jeannie). A friend who called himself the Incredible Red Banana (Michael) joined the group. After the publication of the book many of them dressed up as their 'power animals' on party occasions and many of the Dragon Ship characters such as the Dolphin, Giraffe, Beaver, Dancing Flamingo, Panda Butterfly, Flutter Flump, Banana and others would visit me in my dreams as their fantasy characters.

In 1977 I had a dream of a Cosmic One who told me "I am sitting on the lotus but The lotus is in you". This was when I was following a path of natural ways to feel a heightened energy. I studied Kundalini yoga and the chakras (some sessions were led by Yogi Bhajan) and painted the "Lotus One", which became part of Dodoland. Lotus One lived in the Island of Eyes and told the secret to go home from the land. At the time I was also studying at the Zen Lotus Society and was told by a Zen monk "To paint you must become the painting". I found an ancient Tibetan symbol in a book at the library and since I was attracted to it painted 'Search for Seed'. Thirty five years later when studying Dream Yoga I discovered it was "Om Mani Padme Hung" the chant with mani meaning jewel and padme lotus which is chanted to get into the heart chakra dreams during the night.

Also in 1977 in a dream I met a small boy on a pier and was shown a book. Later I knew this was a prophetic dreams and the boy represented Dr. Dick Mazurek who published "Journey to Dodoland". When the book was being published in Laguna Beach he took me to a pier that was like the dream. As the book was being published I was told by Dream Guides that many people will be touched by the happiness of Flutter Flump. Since he assigned me creative control I included the whole Marshmallow Mountain which the designer wanted to crop out of the story. Also as the book was actually at the printer ready for printing I had a dream of going through a caterpillar 'power' tunnel and coming out to open space where people flew like butterflies. The butterfly became an personal symbol for transformation.

I stopped the press and added words to describe the transformation that was to go with the secret words to come home from "Dodoland". I later painted a large canvas of this dream for the Theatre production of "Dodoland" in New York. I had many dreams later of one thing changing to another and called them my Transformation Dreams. In another important dream in 1977 I received a message that the body is a temple and started to do yoga every day. Staying in the Kootenays then, I woke up one morning from a dream and had a ring of rainbow light on my finger. I wrote the outline for the "Magical Earth Secrets" with the little people of the Rainbow representing the earth, water, sun, air and stars... the essence of elements of life were there and I knew the essential ingredient of love was needed.

In 1978 I was instructed by a dream guide to "write "Magical Earth Secrets" in a teepee. As synchronicity has it my sister Norah told me after this she was planning on staying in a teepee on Kootenay Lake so I joined her and wrote the first draft. I later painted the painting for the story on the same lake in a studio by an ashram. A Dream Guide told me "Dale and you have eagle vision". Dale had been given the name 'White Eagle' by a native shaman and this is how the first character of the "Magical Earth Secrets" came to be. As my dreams often reflected what was going on around me in a Transformation dream I saw Dale, who was the Rainbow Dolphin in the "Dodoland" story, transform and morph into an eagle. In another Transformation dream my mother changed into a white buffalo. Dale actually was later given the name White Buffalo and gifted a Buffalo head dress.

In 1979 I received the message from a Dream Guide "You are the center of the Medicine Wheel and it is turning around you". We did feel in the center of things as Dale and I as Inner City Angel artists led hundreds of workshops with the Inner City children of Toronto. I received many Ontario Arts Council Grants. One such project was the Wandering Spirit Survival School and here the children created a mural of the "Magical Earth Secrets". Many children were encouraged in hundreds of workshops to become their dreams (good dreams of course).

One night in 1979 I had a dream I was in the ocean and when someone was about to drown praying hands came out of the water to help them. Later I painted "Praying Hands" in the" Phoenicorn Fire" story. I seemed to be called to help those in need and in a Guidance Dream in 1980 saw a small disabled boy putting on my Bird Helmet. As synchronicity has it soon after I worked with children at Sunnyview School and later with hearing impaired children. In 1979 while in New York I had a dream that my Bird Helmet was on fire like a Phoenix Bird. Because of the dream when I woke up I phoned the doctor who published the book and said I felt it was most important for the book to go to the poorest children. He then worked his magic and arranged for 6,000 books to be delivered by the Army Core through the Toys for Tots program to children in need for the Christmas of 1979. My powerful dream made this possible.

Birth Dream Cycle 1974 – 1980

Top: Dale & Della – Rainbow Rose Festival, Lotus One , Dr. Dick Mazurek
Middle: Dodo Land, Dragon Ship, Seeing Eye Butterfly, Seed, Bird Helmet
Bottom: Giraffe Lady (Brenda Parres) & Della, Sea of Yourself, Singing Tree

Essence of Life!

Birth Dream Cycle 1974 – 1980

"Birth" painting – oil and egg tempera 2013

Divinely limited in body but Dreams bring Transformation
A place of where Caterpillars change to Butterflies
You visit the Cosmic Lotus One with Chakra Lotuses inside
Where there is a ring of Rainbow Light on your finger
In a teepee you write the "Magical Earth Secrets"
Rainbow Dolphin transforms to Eagle
And Star Bird Mother turns to a While Buffalo
Reminded that the Phoenix when on fire is Reborn
In your Dreams you Mythical Journey.

Reflections from Dream Diaries
Third Cycle- 1981 – 1987
The main theme of the Third Cycle was the Medicine ways.

"You can love and protect the earth"

During this time I had these dreams I call Wisdom Dreams in which I had the overwhelming feeling after, of being advised or guided, to follow a certain path. Sometimes it was a Dream Guide advising me it seemed with wisdom of previous generations and sometimes coming from wisdom I have inside myself. At this time I met Tedrian Chizik who produced Dodoland and he felt so committed to the story that he took the book to Machu Picchu and went to the altar of the Sun God and dedicated the story to the children of the world. After this there were performances of "Journey to Dodoland" at Museo del Barrio and at the Museum of Natural History in New York. He toured with my stories for seven years. One outstanding dream in 1983 was a dream of unicorns jumping out of the sea which inspired me to write the "Phoenicorn Story' with the main character being part unicorn and phoenix. This was my first Spirit Horse dream.

Another recurring dream was my Medicine Wheel Dreams. In these dreams I was In a different position, or situation on a Medicine Wheel or Mandala. Interestingly the dreams seem to relate to what I was doing in my life at the time. During this time I had a dream of sitting right inside the Medicine Wheel We certainly felt in the center of things Medicine Wheel. "Dodoland'"" was performed at the Smithsonian Institute in Washington and Ananda Ashram.

In 1984 in a Wisdom Dream I was told "If things are open it will be more fun". Leaving things open to synchronicity I knew was important. "Journey to Dodoland" was performed at the Cuban Refugee Camps in Pennsylvania and also at the "Magic in Me" Conference in Guatemala where teachers who taught handicapped children. came from all over Central and South America . Dale and I also shared the story in a small village near Lake Atitlan. All were open and we brought fun to those who really needed it. When in Guatemala we visited the sacred site of Tikal . I was told in a dream the Bird Helmet is a 'Symbol of Peace and Goodwill'. We performed at the Sloan Kettering Hospital and the Metropolitan Hospital in NYC the story of Dodoland.

I was told by a dream guide to "teach children about dreams" and I facilitated a Dream Workshop at Christie School in Toronto. Part of the reason I call this the Medicine Cycle is because we were being apprenticed by a shaman who was an unusual blend of European and Indigenous and, at one time, was a student of Dr. Carl Jung in Switzerland. He would often come to me and instruct me in my dreams . One night he told me "to change shape in dreams and shift objects consciously". I decided to fast and had an astounding dream of a giant "White Spirit Rabbit" who was to help children with nutrition. Had many dreams of Power Animols. One was of a Shaman who had a Deer Mask and held a dorje and prophesied the future . We went on a Vision Quest guided by our mentor and I unexpectantly in the wilderness encountered a brown bear that foretold I would be teaching medicine ways. After in my dreams I saw a Shaman who danced with a bear skin. We performed "Dodoland" at the native people's Community Centre in NYC on a Medicine Wheel and in attendance was a 101 year old man who I felt was connected to the bear. To overcome a fear of performing to an audience of over 100 people I took a workshop 'Walking the Firewalk' with Tony Robbins and we had to walk to overcome a fear we had. After doing the Fire Walk the next day I was able to dance the Wise Lotus One in "Journey to Dodoland" at the Brooklyn Academy of Music with an audience of 500 and did not feel nervous. In a Medicine Wheel dream I had been told "You are dancing on the Medicine Wheel" and felt in my performance I was living that dream. I soon, after the storytelling, led an art workshop to women prisoners at Metropolitan Detention Centre for the group called 'Peace thru Culture.' I had collected slides of Nicholas Roerich's painting from NYC The night I came from NYC with Roerich's images I had a 'Mother of the World' dream with her hands stretched out to a light in the cosmos.

One night in Acton Ontario I had a prophetic dream of a bird pecking its way out of the womb. I woke up and wrote the dedication to the "Magical Earth Secrets" story – "After nine months this gift of the rainbow will be given to you" and I did not know at the time of the dream but one of my best friends , Sal , was about to go in labor with a son and coincidentally , though she did not know my dream, called him Rainbow. He became one of our godsons. In yet another Medicine Wheel dream I was told "the Boy Eagle goes with you around the Medicine Wheel." We took the "Magical Earth Secrets" which was the story of the Eagle Child's journey to all the school children in East Harlem and performed at the Third Street Music School for its hundredth anniversary. Our shaman/mentor guided me in designing costumes and direction and I got ideas for costumes from dreams. We included a mermaid for the water part of the story which had been a recurring dream for many years. He also embellished and added new energy to the Bird Helmet. I directed the children's program at the Cape Cod Writers Conference. Many workshops made it possible to share the message we must "love and protect the earth".

In another Medicine Dream Wheel I was told "children should make Medicine Wheels". This dream reflected what Dale was doing as he was leading Medicine Wheel workshops for the Inner City Angels. We got married in 1987 and part of the wedding ceremony was done in a Medicine Wheel at a beautiful spot by Kootenay Lake in which later nearby we built a house. Soon after I attended the "Baby Clown" workshop with Richard Pochinko who used a Shamanic approach to clowning and I dreamt of a butterfly landing on his hand. He developed an approach that he called finding your baby clown and helped me in the work I was doing. The butterfly as a symbol for transformation seemed to reoccur again and again. In 1987 in a Wisdom Dream by a Dream Guide "a transition is made when a mask is put on". Both Dale and I facilitated many workshops with masks – masks as medicine tools for self expression and to help the earth !

Medicine Dream Cycle 1981–87
Thanks to Dale for so many photos taken over many years!

Top: Della, Dale & cousin, Dream Wheel, Macchu Picchu-Peru
Middle: Museum of Natural History, 'Magic in Me' Guatemala, B.A.M.
Bottom: Mask workshop, Dale & Della's wedding, Medicine ceremony

Here's to expression!

Medicine Dream Cycle 1981-87
"Medicine Ways" -acrylic, oil, egg tempera 2013

In your Dreams you find Medicine Ways
A place of New Growth with Dream Birds & Power Allies
You visit ancient sites - Macchu Picchu, Tikal, Palenque.
Where a prophetic Deer Shaman gives you a power song
Told you are a mermaid and to be open
Elder Bear People dance in a circle and ask you to join
And On the Medicine Wheel the Eagle Child guides you
Reminded of White Buffalo & Bird Woman dancing
In dreams the Mother of the World praises the Light

Reflections from Dream Diaries/Dream Wheels
Fourth Cycle- 1988-1994
The main theme of the Fourth Cycle was Wonder

"You can be imaginative and creative."

During this time I had many dreams that seemed to be filled with things so wonderful and magical such as a magical animal, character, person or setting and I so began to think of them as my Wonder Dreams. In 1988 I was told in one such Wonder Dream that "the sound of the flute makes the pineal gland swell." Dr. David Lertzman collaborated in my storytelling of "Magical Earth Secrets" by adding beautiful music. I was also told by a Wonder Guide that "Each child adds a piece to the whole - children are teachers on loving and saving the Earth".

Soon after I was Invited to the Globetree Festival in Stockholm where children shared their feeling on protecting the earth and expressed this in dance and theatre. Some children storytold "Magical Earth Secrets" in the Concert Hall in Stockholm. As I sat in the front hall of the Concert Hall I heard them tell my story and say "I and the Earth are one. I love the Earth". I knew the crucial line that was missing in the story was "I will take care of the Earth" and so this phrase was added and became an important part of the "Magical Earth Secrets" book

In the early 1980's the story of "Magical Earth Secrets" was taken by an agent to NYC and every publisher said protecting the earth was not anything anyone was or would be interested in. I will explain how it became a book - ten years later at a project at the Environment Summit at the Ontario Science Centre Dale, I and Marijke Sluitjer from Holland facilitated an Environment Posters workshop. As I was telling the story "Magical Earth Secrets" Paul George from WWC was in the audience and said afterwards "that is a story I heard David Lertzman tell and I noticed how much the kids loved it and I wanted to publish it". And so in 1990 our second book was born - published by the Western Canada Wilderness Committee - one of the major environmental groups in Canada who have protected many wilderness areas. The story that originally started with the dream of me having a ring of light on my fingers in 1977 was finally now a dozen years later to be published. I was asked to go to Vancouver and work as a designer on the book. To my surprise it became a bestseller in Canada.

In 1991 I was told to "put seeds in the pond and lotuses will grow." A dance of" Magical Earth Secrets" was performed by Maria Formolo Company for the "Celebration of the Environment". Earth Seed, Sweet Water, Love Wind, and Sun Ray were danced, Star Bird sang and the

Eagle Child made by Noreen Crone Findlay sang and danced. I Met
Maria Formolo when doing a storyelling with Vern Harper (Stone)
the Urban Shaman in a teepee in the Kootenays. She saw me tell the
story and said she was going to make a "Celebration of the Environment
and wanted the story to be the focal point of the celebration. I was
taking my Bachelor of Education at Queen's University and
and since I was part of the Artist in Community program was actually
able to make it part of one of my practicums for my Bachelor of Education
which was a small miracle. Seeing the dance performance was like
a dream coming alive.... I could not stop smiling! Dale and I facilitated
many Friends of the Environment projects with environmental themes
and used the "Environmental Activity Guide" which was a companion
to "Magical Earth Secrets"and has many different mandalas in it.
An Art program was done by a woman in Japan called Kazuko Asaba
who told me she was very influenced and inspired by "Magical
Earth Secrets" book and was doing art workshops at the Asaba Art Square
around it. She had the children in Japan become Eagle children.

   In 1992 I was told in a Wonder Dream "To work in the snow."
I started to do ice painting with my mother and these became the
abstract grounds for some of my paintings. I was also guided to make
Dream Hats with kids in the future and I had a dream of doing flying
acrobatics and also flying with a magic carpet. In another Wonder Dream
I was told by a Dream Guide "that everyone has a Spirit Horse".
Also in a "Wonder Dream" I saw an amazing bird and was told by our
mentor that it was a special bird called a Dream Bird. I painted
"Dream Bird" and later added it to "Goodness Sphere" in the
"Miracle Galaxy"and I also included a small boy with a wand that
came from my mentor's dream. In a Wisdom Dream a Dream Guide told
me "a flower growing must die...it is part of life." This prepared me
as our mentor passed to the spirit world.

   During this cycle I was doing art and writing programs through the Inner
City Angeles and grants through the Ontario Arts Council. I visited hundreds
of schools and encouraged the children " to be imaginative and creative."
I had a Transformation Dream of small white tigers turning into colored
elephants. Also in a Wonder Dream a dream guide told me "Inner and outer
space are as powerful as each other", "You can touch a bluebird"
and "You must write poetry". I dreamt of a Palace Angel who held out
a Castle of Dreams with many doors and windows and she said it was possible
to enter any one of them. Later in the Divine Cycle in a workshop
with Dream Shaman Robert Moss and with drumming went through
a purple tunnel and at the end saw a blue Spirit Horse on which I flew to the
Castle of Dreams to receive a gift. This I painted and am sharing with you.
The important message to share with the world and you in this Wonder
 Cycle is to remember your wonder and "be creative and imaginative".

   1

Wonder Dream Cycle 1988 – 1994

Top: Magical Earth Secrets –Sweden, Maria Formolo Dance Company
Middle: Dale & Desiree (mum), Maria, Vern Harper (Stone)
Bottom: Kootenay, Della's Workshops, Japan Asaba Art Square project

Fill the world with Wonder!

Wonder Dream Cycle 1988 - 1994
"Wonder" painting is egg tempera and acrylic washes 2013

In your Dreams you find Wonder
A place where Inner Space is as powerful as Outer Space
You are told everyone has a Spirit Horse & and mine is Unicorn
The Tibetan Wind Horse is the essence of yourself
Seeds planted become lotuses and Angel Guides touch bluebirds
Where Baby White Tigers turn to Baby Elephants
And Acrobats with magic carpets fly to the sunrise sky
Reminded that flowers must die - you still in your dreams
Fearlessly ride your Spirit Horse to the Dream Castle

Reflections from Diaries/Dream Wheels
Fifth Cycle- 1995 – 2001
The main theme of the Fifth Cycle was the Third Eye

"You can find the Cosmic One".

In 1995 I was told in a Wisdom Dream by a dream guide to "manifest art to beauty". In this year Dave Godrey said to me at a "Swiftsure" workshop where Dale and I were learning about the internet "that he was looking for an imaginative story". Dodoland was used to launch the project and thus one of the first electronic magazines for children called "Dodoland in Cyberspace" was born- the place where you could become imaginative and love the earth could be shared. We have had one million people visit.

In 1996 I felt a connection in a dream to the white tiger as a 'Power Animal' and Dream Guide. I painted the white tiger on a paper Bird Helmet design in 1997 and wore it when working with children at a Canadian school in Mexico where I was involved in designing a program to learn English through story, art, dance and music. Laurie McHale and Dale helped me as well in Mexico. Later I wore the hat in the project with children at the Dream Centre and Gapyeong Korea.

In 1998 I had a Medicine Wheel Dream with sacred stones placed in the different directions on the wheel. The Fifth Cycle is a time of travel and adventure and search for the Cosmic One. We lived and worked in England with the intention of being closer to Wales to do research on Dale's book project in which he was searching for an "Inner Merlin". I had dreams of visiting sacred stone circles over many years. I had many reccurring Celtic dreams since the Medicine Cycle. We visited Wales many times as well as Stonehenge, Avebury, Glastonbury, New Grange, Ireland and Cornwall. The book of "Druidical Quest" was being born. I facilitated "Create your own Healing Story" in Holland and Dale shared the Druid manuscripts which were recorded at the turn of the century by a Welshman who called himself " The Last Recorder of the Druid". Dale had inherited them from his mum in 1979 and he travelled researching and trying to understand them. Before this all happened I had a prophetic dream when we were staying at Easalen Institute that the druids were coming. I later did a video called the "Druids are Coming" of us visiting various sacred sites in England, Wales, and Ireland.

In the year 2000 I had surgery for cancer followed with years of recovering. I started to reflect and paint all the qualities needed to survive a crisis which was born later as the book "Miracle Galaxy". I was a patient of Dr. Roger Rogers who founded 'Inspire Health' which has alternatives for cancer. Later he was in my dream when painting the Dream Theme painting "Miracle".

Just seven months after having surgery for cancer, in the summer of 2000, I went to the Kootenays and was in the house we had built there in the mountains by the lake. I had a life-altering mystical experience on the "August Full Moon" and felt my crown chakra and third eye opening and had vision after vision. It was as if my life passed before me in one night and many spiritual guides/sacred spirit teachers/Cosmic Ones came out to help me. I felt the full moon was so strong my chakras were being activated and I was shown my higher self and being called to a deeper life. I received images for paintings and poems that came in what was like a semi-dream state. Some of the images which I gave names to were "Mother Moon", "Swan Goddess", "Ribbon Isis", "Lotus Petal Goddess", "Red Rose Monks", "Merlin Wizard" and "Buddha on a Doorknob". I had a dream of a headband with the Bird Helmet on it and I became the Bird and sprouted large wings and flew. From this day on I could see incredible images in my third eye and felt I had received the message that there are "Cosmic Ones' inside and outside. Afterwards I continued to write and paint the "Miracle Galaxy" story and included the 'Ribbon Isis' in the "Miracle Galaxy" story. This experience seemed to prepare me for many things I would be called on to do later including painting the "Dream Wheels" and painting Aaron Zerah's book – "Spirit Storybooks".

In 2001 had a dream of a man with tattoos that was Maori and he called Dale and my names. This was after we were asked to represent Canada at the World Island Festival in Jeju Island in Korea which had sixteen countries represented. At the Festival I storytold "Magical Earth" and led a workshop with Dale around "Miracle Galaxy" at a school for nurses. I actually saw a group of Maori dancers perform and they looked like the people in my dream. As synchronicity has it we were on the same floor at the hotel with some dancers from Easter Island and they were really excited to see the part in Dale's "Druidical Quest" project about Easter Island being the original home of old Azatlan.

I was told in a Wisdom Dream that I was working from the "Book of Love". Soon after I did a project at the Sundance School in Victoria where I was able to story tell the "Miracle Galaxy" and the students created their own Travel Stories and a large Travel Flower mural. Dream friend Penn Kemp came in and collaborated with me and made "Soundscapes of Sacred Stones Sites" from various parts of the world. The power spots were connected to Dale's Druidical research and since visiting them I included them in my "Miracle Galaxy" story. We showed her photographs of the Sacred power spots and she would intuitively make the most amazing sounds to represent their power of the stones. Some were Stonehenge, Avebury, Boscawen-Un, Chichen Itza, Egypt and New Grange. At the gallery where this happened we had a show of the "Miracle Galaxy" paintings, Dale's work, and a big mural painted by the children of a flower where each petal was a Travel story they created. When the third eye opens and the Cosmic One inside and outside is shown. new worlds and sounds are shown to us.

Third Eye Dream Cycle 1995-2001

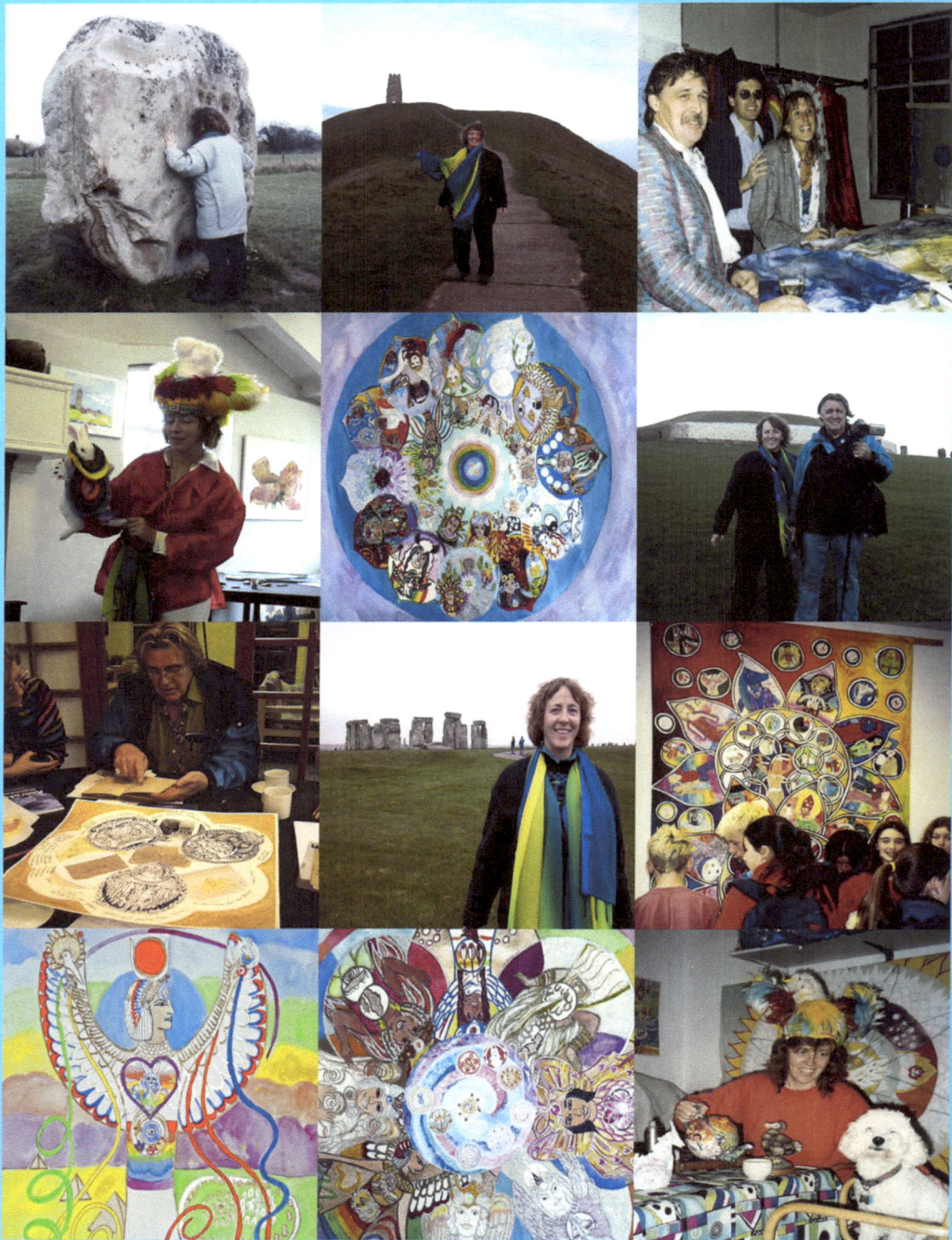

Top: Avebury, Glastonbury, Tom , Sal Williams & Dale Bertrand in studio
Middle: Storytelling Holland, Dale's Druidical Quest, Sundance School
Bottom: Ribbon Angel, Miracle Angels, Della & little dog Bijou

New Worlds are shown!

"Third Eye" – egg tempera and acrylic washes 2013

Divinely limited again but in your Dreams you find Visions
A place called Third Eye where Sacred calls
You visit August Moon – Buddha, Dalai Lama, & Moon Mother
Where Druid Seers help you go on Quests to find Mermaids
You find the Beauty Rose in the middle of a Tibetan Monks Circle
Compassion Lotus Lakshmi and Muse Swan Saraswati witness
And Faces morph , Buddha sits as Isis rythmically Ribbon dances
Reminded Bird Helmet (caduceus) is the Emblem on headband
In your Dreams you become a Bird & sprout Huge Wings and Soar

Reflections from Diaries and Dream Wheels
Sixth Cycle 2002 - 2009
The main theme of the Cycle in Miracles

"You can Self Heal yourself"

In 2002 I had a Wisdom Dream and was told in a dream
"You are to guide people in their spiritual dance." I felt I could fulfill
this dream when I was invited to storytell at the Festival for Children
which was for fifty charities at the South Coast Plaza in Newport Beach,
California. It was powerful time as it was near the home of the late Dr.
Richard (Dick) Mazurek who published the "Journey to Dodoland" twenty
five years earlier and Doug Riseborough who introduced me to Dick.

I had in 2003 a Medicine Wheel Dream and was wearing silver
feathers on my headdress. Also in 2003 in a Wisdom Dream was told
that "those with halos can help." I was able to occasionally communicate
with those people who had departed such as mum and dad, my sister
Donna, and our mentor who I call "Star Bear" who continued to
advise and help me from the Spirit World. I had one dream where
I saw Dick Mazurek who had published "Journey to Dodoland" as well.
I was sad we had not seen more of each other and told him we loved him
for all he had done... various dreams healed relationships. Because
I was grieving with the loss of seven people (two had passed before the
cycle) who were close to me there were periods during this cycle that
I felt 'soul loss' as I did not remember or record my dreams. Finally
communicating with people I loved in the Dream world helped me
feel connected to them again and the dream rememberance drought ended.
My dream of my father was him reaching out his hand to help
me down a steep stairwell, and my mother came as the creative
and loving spirit she always was, and Donna was shown to me as
Crysanthemum who was a Goddess nurturing mother holding and
loving a child in her arms representing compassion and mercy. My dreams
with those departed helped heal relationships and made me feel they
were doing well in the spirit world and I felt my soul coming back to me.

In 2004 in a Prophetic Dream I saw a mermaid statue in a small town
and not having a lot of funds, travelled there by bus to see it. This dream
and other dreams to sacred stone circles inspired me to plan a trip for
Dale and me to various sacred sites in Wales, Cornwall and Ireland.
Dale was researching the Druid manuscripts which in a story he said
he was taught by three woman including his grandmother who called
themselves the 'Three Mermaids'. In Cornwall we saw a mermaid plaque
in a church which used to be an ancient site in Zennor and I felt a
real sense of deja- vu from my dream. Interestingly the mermaid
has always been an important symbol for me and it is an important
part of the story of John Hugh Roberts who wrote the Stone Book
of Knowledge - another incident of life's synchronicity giving direction.

Barbara Tremain used her psychic abilities and showed us places connected to the John Hugh Roberts manuscripts Dale was researching. She would hold the old manuscripts and then seem to know how to guide us. We went to the places where "The Three Mermaids" conducted ceremonies at Land's End and Sacred Stone Circles such as Bocsacwen-Un and the Nine Maidens. I sometimes had the feeling of having been to these places before in my dreams. Also we visited Stonehenge, Avebury, and New Grange in Ireland. After returning we worked on completing Dale's book/journal of the 'Druidical Quest'. At the same time I was working on "Miracle Galaxy" and put the earth homes in the story where Angels in the story lived in the different sacred power spots we were visiting on our trip.

Something from my Dream World happened that helped me paint the setting of the "Miracle Galaxy". One night I woke up and I had a vision of a Milky Way like galaxy. I almost couldn't stop painting until it was done. My hand just kept going around and around in a spiral. I had had a dream previously of the mandala like Spheres where the Angels lived and drew them in as well representing the different chakras. Working on this story was self healing process for me in my cancer recovery and my goal was to share it with the world. I often thought of certain people in my life who were so caring and an inspiration during the healing process and ended up putting up photographs of them around me and painting some of them in the Dream Theme painting of "Miracle".

During this time my twin sister Donna who had been diagnosed with breast and bone cancer was living with us and staying in our house in Nanaimo. She was painting a lot and helped give me ideas for the movement of the Guiding Angels in the Miracle Galaxy story. We drew together the Good Thoughts, Kindness, Intuition and Dream Angel. We went to the Petroglyphs which were the home of the Willpower Angel together and I included her with her rythmic gymnastic ribbons as "Ribbon Isis" for the Creativity Angel in the "Miracle Galaxy". In 2006 my twin Donna passed to the Spirit World. I had many dreams of her afterwards. One I painted.

In 2006 I went to do a teaching project at the Dream Center in Korea. I met someone there who became one of my best friends - Jacquie Howardson. I had a chance to share my stories with hundreds of children. One group was the first group I told the "Miracle Galaxy" story too and they then created their own angels. The Angel concept was new to them and they often chose a teacher to be an angel. I continued when I got back in telling the Miracle Galaxy to children on Vancouver Island and they made Angels to heal themselves and the and the planet. When Miracle Galaxy was published the message "You can heal yourself" went out to the world.

Miracle Dream Cycle 2002- 2008

Top: South Coast Plaza – Festival of Children, Newport Beach
Middle: Mermaid Cornwall, Dream Centre Korea, Mermaid California
Bottom: Paintings for "Miracle Galaxy", Willpower and Dream Angel

Miracles and then a Gratitude Feast!

Miracle Dream Cycle 2002- 2008

"Miracle" egg tempera and acrylic washes 2013

In your Dreams you find needed Miracles
A place of Self- Healing & a place to Spiritually Dance
You visit the Milky Way Galaxy
Where mandela spheres are revealed
You find Silver Feather energy & Healing Food to Survive
Sitting by one you love on earth
And Communicating with family and friends
Reminded also of family and friends Departed
In your Dreams you too can Heal Relationships

Reflections from Diaries/Dream Wheels
Seventh Cycle- 2009- 2015
The main theme of the Seventh Cycle is Divine

"You can co -create with the divine "

In 2010 I had a powerful dream of an indigenous man who with a clap of thunder gave me a necklace and I then saw an eagle and jaguar as Dream Guides. Soon after visited Mexico and I had a Wisdom dream that the ocean was like a snake and I found out from a woman very close to the Huichole that the people saw the snake connected to the movement of the ocean. I really related to the art of the Huichole and also to the Bird Men of Papantla who I saw fly in a ceremony in Puerto Vallarta. When I got back I made a video of the travels to Mexico and the dream. Much later in this cycle had many dreams of power animal allies connected to different chakras in a workhshop with Dream Shaman Robert Moss. .

While in Mexico I dreamt of artist Edward James at a table playing cards and a horse in Art Deco style. He said "I hear you are an artist". Dale and I were on our way to the Edward James Surreal Garden. Edward James was a sponsor of Salvador Dali. In Mexico I also had a prophetic dream of people making small statues for plays. My friend Gloria suggested we go to Foco Tonal in Mexico which has a power spot where the energy seemed to converge and when you stand at the power point and speak words like your name, they were echoed back to you. It was discovered by a man who was a healer; he was shown the location in a dream. There was a castle like building on the property that to my surprise when I entered I saw small statues like the ones I saw in my dream. I had a feeling of deja-vu. I made a video of this dream called Foco Tonal and posted on Vimeo to share this experience with the world.

Twice in 2010 I went to Ubud, Bali and met I Made Sidia. I shared the "Dodoland" story with his dance school students and they did an improv of it. I had a dream and painted monkeys, jungle and shamans. I shared with the world the book "Journey to a Lotus" which was first started in travels to India in the 1970's and I realized when doing it what an influence this period had on my work over many years. I painted many visionary paintings such as "Dream Mermaid", "Twin Flames" and "Transformation". In a dream I visited Mount Kailash after meditating on a photo of it and visualizing being there. This was for a sacred painting which will be shared with the world in "Spirit Storybooks" authored by Aaron Zerah in which in many of the paintings I have been guided by dreams on the details needed. I have often been shown techniques of painting in dreams and visited studios and galleries of other artists work In 2011 Cosm Magazine published "Shaman's Eye" a painting which includes many divine dreams I had to share with the world.

I went to Toronto and led a workshop and then on to New York where I visited our friends Aroon and Indur Shivdasani and then to the Roerich Museum Also I was told in a Wisdom Dream to "Take a raft in a new direction." I analyzed my 36 years of Dream Wheels and then painted seven 'Theme Dream Wheels' in Mexico. This was done to make it possible for my life's dream work to be shared.

In 2012 also because of this dream of Ernst Fuchs with sculptures of spiritual figures, I decided to study and participate in a painting workshop "Old Masters New Visions", in Vienna with Philip Rubinov Jacobson whose mentor is Ernst Fuchs. I met many Visionary artists at the 'Uncommon Visions' show which Professor Philip was curating and was able to arrange for some artists to be in this Dream book like Liba, Jody, De Es, Peter, Cynthia, Kuba, Daniel, Vesna and Andrew. In 'Dream Wheels' their "Conscious"art will be shared with the world. Following my dream I visited the Chapel that Ernst Fuchs painted in Klagenfurt and was surrounded by spiritual figures. I did a video of my spiritual pilgrimage to Klagenfurt.

I had a dream 'of creative artists painting and being creative together' and helped manifest two artists retreats in Bali In the first one my sister Norah Burford was Event Planner with Philip Rubinov Jacobson teaching painting , myself teachingan 'Inspiration' class, Dale teaching Medicine Wheels and Guest Artists De Es and Wolfgang Widmoser. The theme was "Transformation". Creative artist being inspired together also happened with "Magical Earth Secrets"as it became a play in Japan with a creative group in 2013.

In 2013 I also was asked by Julie Lieberman who was a performer and one time Musical Director of the "Journey to Dodoland" show in New York City to be a Contributing Writer for the "New town Peace Park Handbook" and shared the "Kindness and Good Thought Angels from the "Miracle Galaxy" as these were the Angels I was told in a dream to be the most helpful in this tragic situation. Liba Waring Stambollion, from Paris, asked me to be a Poet in the book "Divining the Dream" with 61 artists and 26 poets which I have been thrilled to be part of this important project. I met Robert Moss during this cycle and went on many dream journeys with his drumming includ-ing going in a 'power tunnel' and when coming out meeting my Spirit Horse or Wind Horse -'the essence of ones self'. In 2013 I found one night I needed color in my dream and said "rainbow" and a rainbow appeared.

In 2014 we will hold the "Spirit of Writing and Art" in Ubud Bali and I will show the Dream Wheel paintings at a gallery in Ubud in collaboration with an artist in Bali – Karja. I will help others to create their Creative Dream Wheels – Inner Dream Mandalas. For the world vison in this cycle I have and will continue to explore and share with the world the places where humans and the divine co-create. At the completion of the Seventh Cycle of seven years I know there will be a new beginning. I am feeling an eighth cycle called Oneness.

Divine Dream Cycle 2009–2015

Top: Bird Men of Papantla, Foco Tonal, Dale & Della in Mexico
Middle: Arthoff Show, Made Sidia, Roerich Museum, Fuchs Chapel,
Bottom: Spirit Storybooks, Old Masters/New Visions, Retreat Bali

A time of Fruition!

Divine Dream Cycle 2009-2015
"Shaman's Eye" watercolor & acrylic 2011

In your Dreams you find the Divine
A place where the Human and Divine co-create
Where Eagle, White Tiger, Jaguar, Elephant & Deer Dance
You visit Dream Shaman, Blue Buddha, & Druid Wizard
Where there is Validation of dreams value
You continue to Honor your Dreams of prophecy & guidance
And help others to Accept, Manifest & Honor Dreams Gifts
Reminded that Dreams are Wise and very Precious
In your Dreams you Can and Do Change World Essence

I had a dream of a ring of rainbow light on my finger in the Medicine Cycle (1977) and wrote the essence of "The Magical Earth Secrets". During the Wonder Cycle in 1990 it became a book and Kazuko Asaba saw it and did art workshops around the story. Now she has spearheaded it as a play produced by Designer Ruu*Ruu.

Eagle Child Yauhiro Takeda

Kazuko Asaba, Aki Noguchi & Ruu*Ruu

Everyone in the the Magical (Majcal) Rainbow show. Photographs by Masanao Showjit Sugyama, Ruu*Ruu, and Tehran Nakayama

I am honored to have Magical Earth Secrets made into a play. This is the 100% PARADE group who performed the story at the Kanazatabunko Festival and in Tokoyo in 2012. The story came from a dream and with many peoples efforts turned into a beautiful dream coming alive! Thanks all!

Right Earthseed Ricky Rusi Nishzawa, Sweetwaters Yuhki Oomoto & Satri Abe
Star Bird - Ishio Yuki Spring with children - Tara Kashahara .. thanks everyone

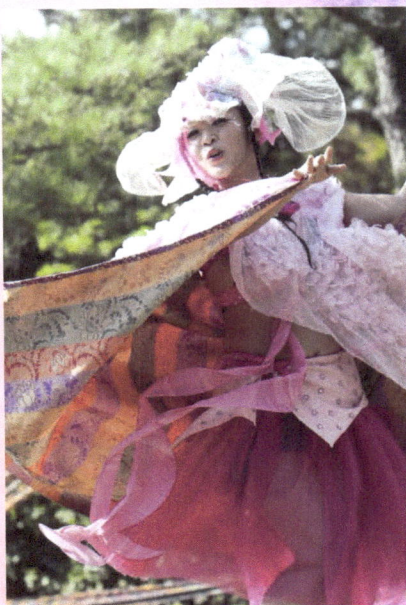

Love Wind - Momo Nakagawa   Sun Ray by Kazyuki Mitani   Wise Woman by Kazuko Asaba

Find Your 'Creative Dream Wheel' – 'Inner Dream Mandala' ('Inner Life Mandala')

Go into the inner sanctuary of your confident, creative and unique self and find out how discovering your inner world and mythic story but remaining grounded with compassion you can enhance your life and make a difference in the world. Write or tell a story, paint a picture , dance or sing your personal dream. Each part is like a portal to learn more about yourself. Enter the doorway. Put four quadrants that will represent the four directions and four different parts of your life. Choose four photos of you to reflect on for these quadrants. Record three of the most memorable dreams you have had. Your first Mandala Wheel may be a collage with photos, the second an art piece All parts become your own personal "Inner Dream Mandala" or "Inner Life Mandala". You can have a fifth part and make wishes for the future and show what you want to visualize for yourself.

1. Initiation– Map your transformational challenges. What is a time you felt phyical, mental (crisis of consciousness) or divine limitations. something felt stuck. Often a door opens..what door opened for you? This will be from time born and look into future.

2. Birth – Have you had a dream of transformation? Choose a symbol from your dreams (or create one) to represent breaking free of limitations. Visualize, then collage, draw or write .

3. Medicine Ways – What is a power animal / nature guardians you have had in your dreams? Consider the animals/birds of the medicine wheel If you did not have a dream of this –what is your favourite tree and animals? Visualize, then collage, draw or write.

4. Wonder – Have you had a dream of a positive imaginative character or creative place in your dream? Visualize, draw or write.

5. Healing – Have you had someone offer a healing in a dream when you were not well? They are like hero and heroines of healing. –it may be those who care/love you. Visualize, collage, draw/write.

6. Vision – Have you had a sacred spirit being visit you in a dream or in your third eye vision? If not – what sacred spirit being (Cosmic One) would you like to have visit you? Visualize, collage, draw or write the Cosmic One.

7. Divine –Have you felt "something divine" in a dream? Divine as eternal and based in truth. Visualize, draw or write.

Find your

Inner Dream

Mandala!

Write a Dream Poem
How do you fly in your dreams?

We all have ways of flying in our dreams.
What way do you fly? Paint or write a poem about
your flying dream. In my Flying Poem each line is a
title of a dream I have had.

"Eagle with high pitched sound
Bird Whistle is the sound of God
Your aura is friendly for birds to rest
Let the wind take you flying
Bird Helmet is healing caduceus
Gold light pouring from the helmet
You are the Bird Helmet
Give yourself the gift of vision
Spread your wings and fly!"

'Over the Sea of Yourself' – Della Burford

We come together to dream!

to find Who You Are.
to find Solutions
to find Power Animals
to find travel to New Places
to find the Imaginary
to find the Cosmic One
to find the Muse
to find Visions
to find Self-healing
to find the Divine
to find Angels and Doorways
to find Emotions and Beauty
to find Dream Galleries and Dream friends
and to express and Honor our Dreams
for Self Growth, Humanity and the World

'Transformation' – Della Burford

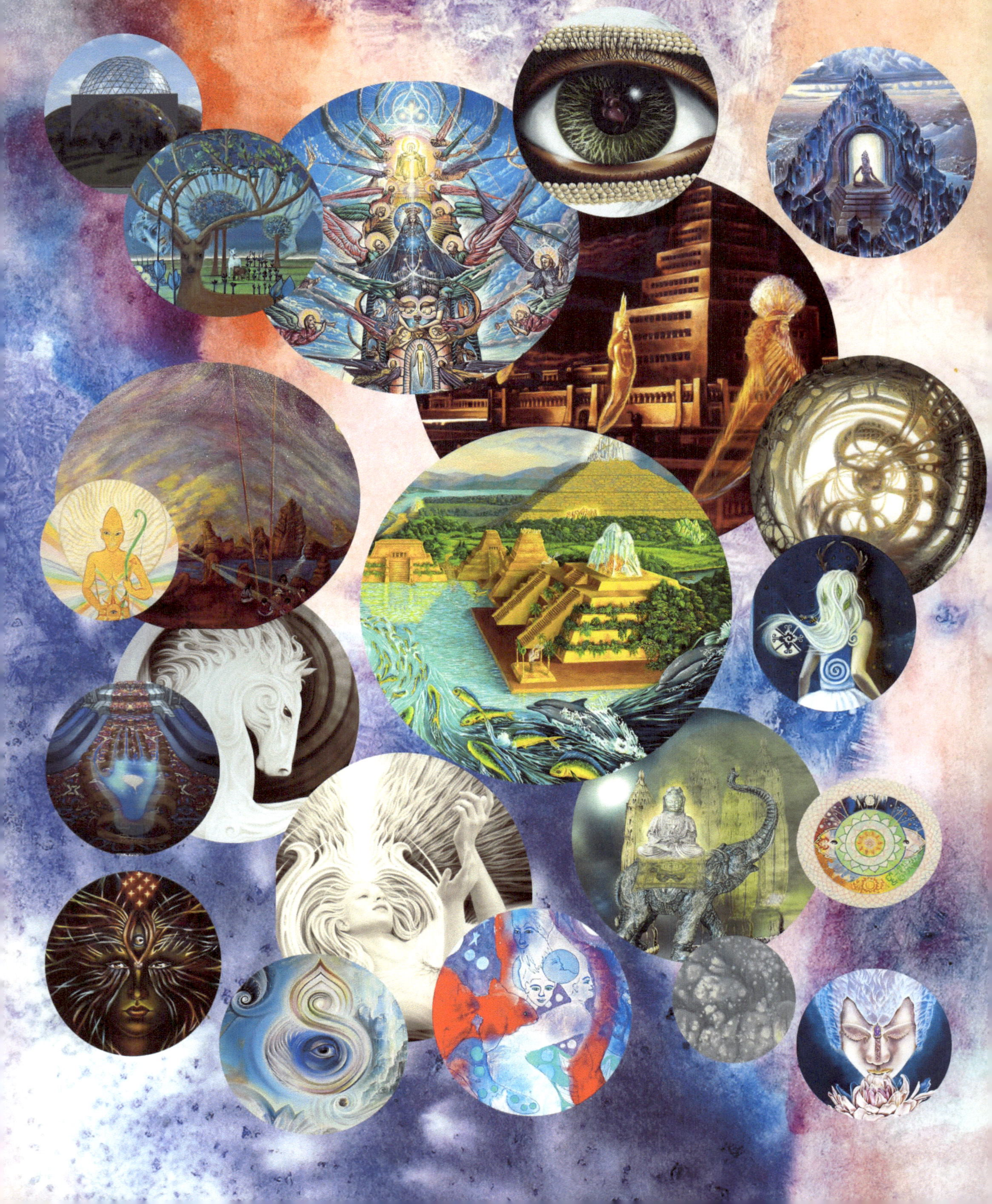

We come together to dream!

Dream to find Who You Are!

Look into your dreams and you can find out more about who you are – make a dream painting of your own! Dream Mermaid below was painted from my dream.

Each line of the poem "We come together to Dream" is from different International Artists who have painted from their dreams.

'Dream Mermaids' – Della Burford

Dream to find Solutions !

When travelling in Guatemala we discovered
the children had these tiny 'trouble dolls'
that they told a problem to. They put the dolls
under their pillows and during the night when
sleeping they would find a solution in their dreams.
Liba Waring Stambollion in her painting is saying,
"That the choice to be here in this mysterious
experience is so full of beauty and also pain
but it is mine. And I manifest beauty in
body mind and spirit and it is good."

'The Choice' – Liba Waring Stambollion

Dream to find
your Spirit Horse!

I was told in a dream that everyone has their own spirit horse. It is like our breath and the wind that blows around us with life. It can be many kinds of horses. I have had many variations, the latest being Pegasus who was my dream companion when travelling to Austria. Was excited to meet Andrew Gonzalez there who painted Pegasus beautifully. Draw or paint your own Spirit Horse to take you to higher realms!

'Pegasus' – Andrew Gonzalez

Dream to find your Power Animal!

Everyone has different Power Animals for dream guides. You can find strength from them. Austrian artist Vesna Krasnec has dreamed and painted the deer. Dream shaman Robert Moss says in Active Dreaming "I found in many ancient and indigenous traditions antlers are a symbol of spiritual authority because they grow above the physical head, reaching towards the realm of the spirit. They signify regeneration because they die and grow back bigger than before."

'Deer Dream' – Vesna Krasnec

Dream to find travel to New Places!

In dreams we are able to travel anywhere,
to another part of the world, to
another planet or imaginary world...
anything in possible.
Artist Cynthia Re Robbins had
a dream of being led by a leaping
dorado fish to her original home, the
landscapes were surrounded by water.
She painted her 'Golden Dream'.

'Sueno Dorado' – 'Golden Dream' – Cynthia Re Robbins

....two realities overlapping.

Spiralling inside himself, artist Peter Gric travelled to new dimensions by using his imagination. He was playing around with two forms when he saw a landscape – or an altered perception of a landscape in a space warp kind of situation: two realities coming together, overlapping and interfering with each other in the fashion of a "paradigm shift experience", showing a view behind the horizon.

'Interference Zone' – Peter Gric

Dream to find the Imaginary..

In dreams the power of imagination
is endless. I found a lot of ideas
for 'Journey to Dodoland' in my dreams!

'Dodo Land Map' – Della Burford

...places where creativity reigns!

The imaginary place called Nature
Wheel Island in 'Magical Earth Secrets'
and the core idea for the galaxy and the
Mandala Spheres for the story of the
'Miracle Galaxy' came from dreams.
Dreams can reveal insight that can
heal body, mind and soul.

Imagination in dreams is endless!

'Nature Wheel Island'   'Miracle Galaxy' – Della Burford

Dream to find Cosmic one !

After travelling in India and being told in a
dream 'The lotus is inside of you' I painted
the Lotus One. Dale also discovered
a Celtic Cosmic One inside of him that was like
Merlin the magician. Every one is different. The
Cosmic boy/girl .. man/woman is inside everyone..
The painting on the right was inspired
by a sketch Dale did called 'Ancient One'.

'Lotus One' – Della Burford

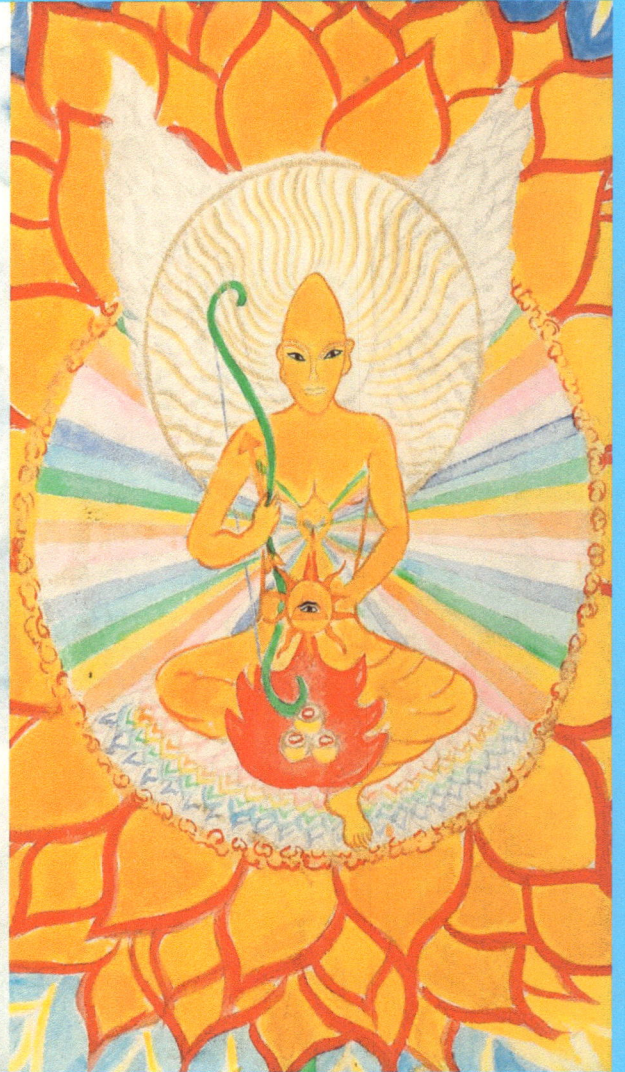

'Sun Ray' – Della Burford
Inspired by Dale's sketch

Dream to find a Muse!

Sometimes in dreams you can visit a wise
one or place for guidance.
Here Daniel Mirante in a dream visited
a colored crystal mountain that clarified,
healed, and restored him. As he dreamt
he heard celestial musicians and was visited
by a spiritual muse. A muse is something
or someone who inspires you.

'Song of Vajra' – Daniel Mirante

Dream to find Visions

Visions illuminate something important for our growth. They are not readily seen by the physical eyes. Rolland Proulx is an artist who states: "My path is the path of beauty. Through my work I strive to communicate the inherent mystery of the living fire breathing in and through all things where past, present and future are synthesized harmoniously & crystallized into a living magnet."

'Mother of the World' by Rolland Proulx

and find more Visions !

In our visions in our dream world we can see our inner self. Artist Jennifer Michelle Long states "Yes...in my dream I was looking in the mirror and I saw this transparent headdress mask when I saw myself- it was like this soul reflection.. this inner being which looked like something I had doodled before in a drawing, ...and in this dream I came to the realization that it was in me. "

'Heightened Sight' by Jennifer Michelle Long

Dream to find Self-healing

Self-healing ideas can come to help you when in need in dreams. Irene Vincent dreamt she was in a Mayan ruin and because of the dream went to Tikal. When she came home she became sick but had a dream of a circle of shamans who came to help her. She looked in a book when she woke up and found the shaman was Huichole - a very special tribe from Mexico. She painted this painting to bring you into her dream.

'Planetary Alignment for Dreamtime'
Irene Vincent

Dreams to find the divine!

Dreams can give you guidance.
Kuba Ambrose in a dream
looked thru an album of another
artist and saw an image of a great
tower. Later he was doing a
painting of a vision that Catherine
Emmerich had and realized
it was the same tower from his
dream. This coincidence and
dream was profound for him.

'Mystery of the Restoration' - Kuba Ambrose

Dream to find Doorways!

Doorways can be opened in dreams
to new ideas. Mark Lee who is a Welsh
born nomadic dreamer searches
for doorways to quests that have
meaning and magical adventures.

'Doorway of Hearts' by Mark Lee

More Doorways!

You can travel in dreams
Della wanted to paint Kailash so
meditated on it before sleeping and
went there in her dreams.

'Swan Buddha' by Della Burford

Dream to find Angels!

Angels can come in dreams
to help guide you through
adversity when you need it.
Andrew Gonzalez portrays
the angels beautifully in his
paintings.

'Yemanja' – Andrew Gonzalez

... birth of a new Angel!

In painting we can also create new things. When artist Jody Florman was meditating and painting she gave birth to a new angel, maybe this was the angelic part of herself showing its face.

'Birth of an Angel' – Jody Florman

Dream to find Emotions!

Gabriella Garza Padilla has recorded her dreams for decades. When she paints rather than paint from her dreams she paints from a state she reaches through self – hypnosis. She finds repetition encourages this. She says about her painting: This painting is about the emotion we put when we are daydreaming. Putting our heart in our visions, in that hologram we see while daydreaming. We have wings in our mind if the emotion is where our vision is, and we will manifest that vision in real life. Emotion is key when we are envisioning something.

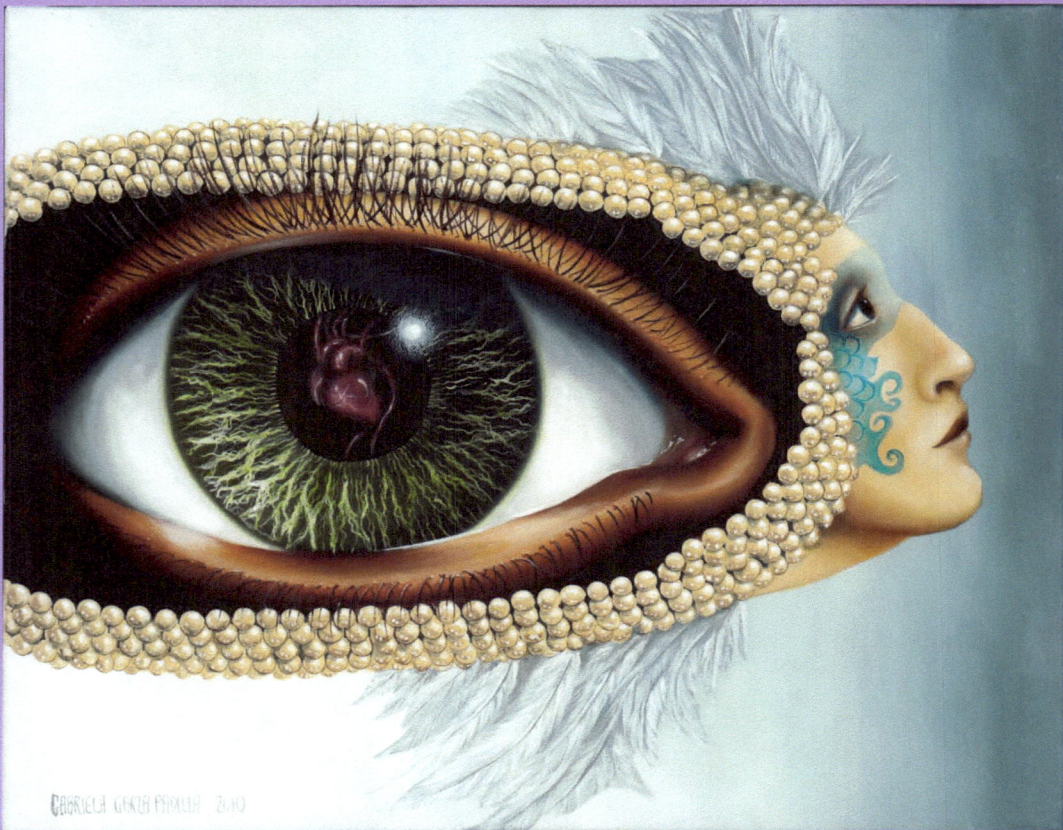

'Daydream' by Gabriela Garza Padilla

Dream to find beauty!

"The eye in the center of a swirling energetic infinity loops symbolic of the belief that the perceiver is always in the sacred center of their ever-evolving experience. Thus, "beauty is in the eye of the beholder". One is always drawing experiences toward themselves, and interpreting life through their own personal lens. Relativity is the awareness that all beings are creating reality individually and collectively" Aloria and David

'Relativity' Aloria Weaver and David Heskin

Dream to find Dream Galleries!

Sometimes words of wisdom come
in dreams and things happen that
give us new knowledge.
De Es, an artist from Austria, told
me he often has dreams of visiting
galleries. I was thrilled as these
are also dreams I have, of visiting
different artists and galleries of their
paintings. I was fascinated to see the
simulation of the inside of his
'Peace Dome' which to me is a
beautiful gallery of his painting
and an offering of beauty for the world.

'Inside the Peace Dome gallery' De Es Schwertberger

Dream to find Dream Friends!

Philip Rubinov Jacobson in his book 'Promethean Flame – Rekindling and Re-visioning the Creative Fire ' says "The intuitive knowledge of artists and non-artists alike is expressed through feelings, dreams, symbols, and fantasies." In 'Drinking Lightning – Art Creativity and Transformation' he says "The dreams can become a kind of clear vision and an increasingly meaningful way of receiving guidance for anyone." In our dreams we can journey to new inspiring places and meet guides and new dream friends.

'The Mission – the Journey'– Philip Rubinov Jacobson

Meeting 'Dream' Artists in Vienna 2012

1. Top L Dream Consultation re book by Prof Philip Rubinov Jacobson
2. Top R Group photo Fuchs Villa Vienna.. many International Artists
3. Middle Della and De Es Swertberger – Austrian artist
4. Vesna Krasnec (Austrian artist) and Della Bottom L
5. Bottom middle Liba Stambollion Paris (Divining the Dream) and Della
6. Della painting at 'Old Masters New Visions' Vienna 2012
   (Thanks to Peter Gric & others for the various photos)

Della Burford

B.Sc, B.Ed , N.Y.S.I.D.

Della's life is a example of dreams coming true and she encourages others to do the same in their lives. Della leads workshops internationally. A former college teacher she is a storyteller, life-long dream adventurer and author, painter of "Journey to Dodoland," "Magical Earth Secrets" ,"Miracle Galaxy", "Journey to a Lotus" , the collaboration "Spirit Storybooks" and now "Dream Wheels". She facilitates many workshops in art and writing including "Creating your own Myth" and "Inner Dream Mandalas".

Dreams have always played a large role in the development of her paintings and books. Many stories /images that came from dreams were manifested in plays such as "Journey to Dodoland." and "Magical Earth Secrets" which were performed for seven years to over 100,000 children in New York, California, Guatemala, Sweden, Canada and Italy in such venues, as the Museum of Natural History,Staten Island Children's Museum, St. Peter's Church at Citicorp, 3rd Street Music School, Brooklyn Academy of Music, and the Discovery Theatre at the Smithsonian Institute in Washington. Della co-directed the "Dodoland" and "Magical Earth Secrets" Productions and was co-playwright & costume designer. Her stories have also been shared in hospitals, prisons, and with thousands of underprivileged children On the internet Dodoland has been visited by a million people. In 2013 "Magical Earth Secrets" was made into a play in Japan by 100% PARADE.

The book "Miracle Galaxy" was created to help those in need face a crisis. The Galaxy itself and Mandala Spheres came to her in a dream. Della was honored to have this story shared with many cancer patients at Inspire Health and other organizations helping people with cancer. Also part of this story was shared in the "Newtown Peace Park Handbook".

After having a powerful dream of Ernst Fuchs Della studied the 'mische' painting technique' with Master Painter Philip Rubinov Jacobson in Austria to help portray her dreams. She led an Inspiration workshop in Bali and in 2014 will teach art and writing there . In 2013 she felt privileged to do a Dream Workshop with Dream Shaman Robert Moss in Vancouver and connect with other dreamers. In 2014 she will launch the "Dream Wheels" book and facilitate a workshop in Bali at the Karja Art Space.

Della's work is for one's self development, our Mother Earth, all of humanity and spirit. Remembering and honoring her dreams has helped and is still helping her fulfill her true destiny in life. She wishes in sharing this book of "Dream Wheels" with you will be able to do the same in your life.

Thank you so much!

I want to thank all those who have helped fulfill
my dreams, but first to my loving husband Dale Bertrand,
and all the family of Burfords who have always stood by me.
Thanks to Tom & Sal and all of the Williams family and so
many other very good friends who I feel so privileged to have
as part of my life. Thank you everyone.

Thanks to Mark Jenkins who in listening to my Dream
Journey helped me crystallize how to tell part of my story.

Also to the late Dr. Dick Mazurek & Doug Riseborough,
who in helping launch "Dodoland" set the stage for me
believing dreams can come true. Thanks to the Inner City
Angels and Ontario Arts Council who helped me share my work

Thanks to the Western Canada Wilderness Commitee
for believing in my story "Magical Earth Secrets". Imaginations
Unlimited including Merian Soto , Julie Lyonn Lieberman, in
New York and Maria Formolo of Formolo Dance Association and
Noreen Crone- Findlay who storytold and the musicians
who were part of the production in Edmonton. I also thank
Kazuko Asaba, Ruu*Ruu and all the people and musicians
in the play that was made of "Magical Earth Secrets" in Japan

My gratitude to Tenzin Wangpal Rinpoche for Dream Yoga ,
Star Bear for guidance & Robert Moss for dream knowledge and
inspiration. Thanks to Patricia Garfield for her "Creative Dreaming"
book which I was introduced to in the 1970's and was inspiring.

I also want to thank my mum, Desiree Burford for encouraging
my creativity and my sister Norah for organizing the Bali events
which will include a show of "Dream Wheels" at the Karja Art Space.

Thanks to my brother Glen and his family for helping with
so many things over many years, and Jacquie Howardson,
Jeannie Thomas and Dale for help in editing.

Thanks to everyone at Inspire Health for their alternatives.

Thanks to all my writing friends and the artists who contributed their
beautiful paintings with energy to this book

I am sorry if I have forgotten someone and appreciate everyones help.

Thanks to all my Dream Guides who have guided me in my
dreams and Dream Allies who have helped with visions. Each day
I learn a little more about dreams and dreaming.

"Create from your dreams! "
with love, Della

www.ingramcontent.com/pod-product-compliance
Lightning Source LLC
Chambersburg PA
CBHW060811090426
42737CB00002B/33